Original title:
The Crab's Sidestep

Editor: Jessica Elisabeth Luik
Author: Kaido Väinamäe
ISBN HARDBACK: 978-9916-86-485-2
ISBN PAPERBACK: 978-9916-86-486-9

Submarine Steps

Beneath the waves, where shadows play,
Mysterious paths in blue array,
A world unseen by surface eyes,
In depths where ancient secrets lie.

Through coral towers, fish parade,
In colors bright, yet softly fade,
Their whispers lost in ocean's song,
Where silence reigns, yet pulses strong.

Glimmers dance on sandy floors,
Reflecting light from far-off shores,
In the stillness, echoes hum,
Of journeys made, and those to come.

Seagrass sways in gentle sway,
Marking paths where currents lay,
Each step a story, silent, deep,
In the ocean’s heart, memories sleep.

Submarine steps, a silent quest,
In twilight’s realm, where souls find rest,
A dance beneath, where dreams abide,
In the ocean’s arms, horizons wide.

Saltwater Dance

Beneath the waves, where secrets sing,
Mermaids twist in a coral ring.
Their fins flash bright, a graceful dance,
In moonlit depths, they now prance.

Anemones sway with the tide,
Crabs join in, no need to hide.
Starfish twirl in sandy beds,
Seaweed curls around their heads.

Crustacean Circles

Beneath the blue, in shadows cast,
Crabs and lobsters have a blast.
With pincers keen, they form a line,
In the dance, they intertwine.

Rocky homes echo tales so grand,
Each claw click, a command.
Barnacles cling to ancient wood,
Time's embrace understood.

Waves and Wiggles

The sea's surface ripples with glee,
Dolphins leap in wild spree.
With every splash, a playful cheer,
Oceans sing, the sky is near.

Jellyfish drift in rhythmic trance,
Caught within the sunlight’s glance.
Their ghostly forms, a ballet true,
In the waters, they renew.

Deep Sea Jig

In twilight zones, the fish ignite,
Bioluminescent light.
Silent currents guide the crew,
Through the abyss, they pursue.

Eels wind through cavern veins,
Silent whispers in the chains.
Anglerfish with lantern bright,
Lure the dance within the night.

Seaside Waltz

Waves in rhythm, dance so free,
Moonlight shines across the sea,
Seagulls cry in twilight's haze,
Golden sands in soft embrace.

Gentle breeze whispers through,
Stories of old, ancient and true,
Footprints trace a fleeting song,
Tides sing out, where hearts belong.

Stars above in silent plea,
Reflect in waves, a glowing sea,
Nature's waltz beneath the skies,
Endless dance where spirit flies.

Saltwater Whirl

Foam and brine in swirling dance,
Ocean’s heart in vivid trance,
Currents twist in wild ballet,
Nature’s pulse at break of day.

Crashing waves in joyful leap,
Secrets of the deep they keep,
Laughter echoes off the shore,
Saltwater whispers evermore.

Sunrise paints the sea in gold,
Mysteries of the world unfold,
Tides in motion, never still,
Life in ever-changing thrill.

Shoreline Pirouette

Sand and sea in tandem play,
Greeting dawn of a new day,
Shells and stones in patterns laid,
By the dance of moonlit spade.

Whirling winds in seaside glee,
Spiraling through the open sea,
Graceful arcs on horizon’s edge,
Nature’s art in silent pledge.

Footsteps trace a fleeting grace,
Transient as the ocean’s face,
Every turn and gentle spin,
Etching moments deep within.

Night Waves Waltz

Stars above in scattered light,
Guide the waves through velvet night,
Oceans hum a lullaby,
Beneath the wide and starry sky.

Moon ascends, a silver queen,
Over waters, calm and serene,
Ripples waltz with soft embrace,
Casting shadows on the face.

Quiet whispers fill the air,
Songs of love both faint and fair,
Every wave, a touch so sweet,
In this dance where hearts meet.

Tidal Tango

The waves embrace, a dance divine,
Their swirls and dips, a trace refined,
To moonlit rhythms, they align,
On liquid floors, their steps confined.

Each crest a curve, each trough a glide,
They move as one, with naught to hide,
A silent song within the tide,
Where sea and sky in waltz reside.

Upon the shore, their tale unfurls,
A dance of water, shimm'ring pearls,
With every turn, the ocean swirls,
As passion through the current whirls.

The sandy stage, their fleeting home,
A canvas vast, where lovers roam,
They twirl beneath the starry dome,
In Tidal Tango, free to roam.

Littoral Line Dance

The shoreline calls with quiet grace,
Where waves and wind in rhythm chase,
A pattern forming, soft embrace,
As sands of time find their own pace.

Footsteps trace a subtle line,
Along the coast, where currents shine,
Each step a tick of nature's time,
In dance where land and sea combine.

With toe and heel, the dance goes on,
A duet lasting until dawn,
Each breaker singing its own song,
Where ocean's whispers sail along.

The seaweed sways, caught in the tune,
Beneath the sun or somber moon,
Their movements linked to ancient rune,
In Littoral Line Dance, they commune.

Seaside Footwork

Bare feet imprint the sandy shore,
A dance begun, a silent roar,
Where ocean's edge invites and more,
The Seaside Footwork to explore.

Each step a kiss upon the land,
Embracing where the waters gland,
In rhythms only few understand,
A ballet where the seas expand.

The shells and stones become the drums,
Their resonance in tidal hums,
A chorus where the coastline strums,
To footsteps tracing where love comes.

Between the grains of ancient tales,
Each footprint tells as movement sails,
In Seaside Footwork, spirit trails,
Where heart and earth intertwine veils.

Echoes in the Tide

In murmured waves, the echoes rise,
Of ancient times and starry skies,
The whispers of the tide make ties,
To songs of old and hidden cries.

Each wave a messenger from afar,
Bringing tales of where we've are,
Their cadence like a soft guitar,
In symphony beneath the bar.

The rocks retain the echoes' tune,
Holding secrets of the moon,
Their resonance a gentle croon,
To rhythms cast from dune to dune.

On shores where silence finds a guide,
The heartbeats of the ocean slide,
Through Echoes in the Tide, they bide,
In watery prose where dreams reside.

Saltwater Strut

Waves that crash in rhythmic dash,
On shores of golden hue.
Dance of foam, in ocean's home,
Beneath a sky so blue.

Shells do twirl in tidal swirl,
Seagulls' calls collaborate.
On silky sand, where waters land,
Nature's ballet instigate.

Starfish glide on seabed's ride,
While crabs in sidestep prance.
Coral fans, with graceful spans,
Weave an aquatic dance.

Dolphins leap in joyous sweep,
Through vernal liquid air.
On moonlit nights, where beams ignite,
The strut is everywhere.

Oceans hum with ancient drum,
A deep and timeless plea.
In waves they trot, in bubbles caught,
Saltwater's melody.

Shoreline Serenade

Soft whispers of waves caress the shore,
Gentle murmurs greet once more,
A symphony of salt and sand,
Nature's orchestra, grand and grand.

Seagulls call in the morning light,
A chorus sung to greet the bright,
With each note that rises high,
A love song to the open sky.

Pebbles dance beneath the tide,
Secrets in their hearts confide,
Every ripple tells a tale,
Of ancient mariners who did sail.

The shoreline sings in sweet refrain,
A melody both wild and tame,
With every crest and gentle fall,
The ocean speaks, embracing all.

Coastal Choreography

Footprints trace the sandy dance,
A ballet of chance and circumstance,
Into the waves they stride and sway,
Lost in rhythm, night and day.

Seaweed strands like dancers' hair,
Tangle in the ocean's care,
Twirl and spin in currents' clasp,
Held in nature's tender grasp.

Tidal pools in mirrored grace,
Reflecting sky and dream's embrace,
In shallow depths, life pirouettes,
A watery world's silhouettes.

Crabs scuttle in their quick ballet,
Shells clink in the evening's sway,
On this stage of endless blue,
The dance continues, old and new.

Moonlit Marine Ballet

Under the moon's soft, silver light,
The ocean sparkles, pure delight,
Waves perform in glistening rows,
A ballet only the night sea knows.

Stars above like audience wide,
Watch the dance, and then confide,
Secrets held in cosmic grace,
Reflected in the ocean's face.

Dolphins leap in arcs so grand,
Their splashes paint the moonlit sand,
Each movement, fluid, free, and bright,
Choreographed by the quiet night.

Silent whispers of the deep,
Guard the dreams the waters keep,
In the moonlit marine ballet,
The ocean's heart will ever sway.

Ebb and Flow

The tide retreats, it hides away,
Only to return one day,
In endless cycles, back and forth,
A dance of south, a dance of north.

Sandcastles crumble, then renew,
Built again by morning’s dew,
With each ebb and flow of time,
The shore sings its soothing rhyme.

Driftwood journeys far and near,
Tells of places once so dear,
A sailor’s tale of wanderlust,
Carried by the ocean’s trust.

Ebb and flow, the constant beat,
The heart of oceans at our feet,
In harmony with Luna's glow,
Forever in the ebb and flow.

Rhythms of Rocks

In caverns deep where shadows creep,
A heartbeat echoes clear.
The granite hums, the marble drums,
A symphony to hear.

Quartz crystals chime in rhythmic time,
With sandstone's soft refrain.
Echoes aglow, of long ago,
In nature's own domain.

Fossils trace the ancient grace,
Of dances wrought in stone.
Erosion's roll on canyon's soul,
Shapes time in monotone.

Basalt's song both loud and long,
Volcanic voices rise.
The earth beneath, in subtle seethe,
With vibrant lullabies.

Mountains croon a mystic tune,
Strata harmonize.
From peaks to streams, in geologic dreams,
The rock dance never dies.

Undersea Pirouette

Beneath the waves where light does dance,
Mermaids circle in a trance.
Coral castles, bright and grand,
Pose as their stage, a magic land.

Whales hum low, a rhythmic base,
Each twirl and twist, a fluid grace.
Fish do glitter, scales so bright,
Adding spark to the silent night.

Jellyfish float in glowing streams,
Echoes of the moon's soft beams.
Starfish cling to rocks below,
Watching wonders they will never know.

The ocean holds this secret art,
A symphony within the heart.
Currents guide the dancers' feet,
In this world where sea and beauty meet.

Submarine Footwork

Beneath the swells where silence dwells,
A hidden world abounds.
With dance so grand, on ocean's sand,
The sea's ballet resounds.

Low they move in grooves of blue,
Mantas sweep with grace.
In depths profound, they swirl around,
A liquid artful chase.

Octaves soft in twilight croft,
Submarines glide in sync.
Glimmers bright through shadows' light,
In ocean's deepest rink.

Treasure chests in sea's contests,
With ships long ago sunken.
Amidst the might, in muted light,
The footwork is unbroken.

Swirling kelp in rhythmic help,
To currents' whispered call.
A dance so deep, in oceans' keep,
The submarine enthrall.

Beach Ballerina

Morning sun on golden sands,
Soft waves caress the dancer’s hands.
Seagulls cry an alto tune,
In sync with dawn, a soft monsoon.

Barefoot steps leave marks in time,
Tracing rhythms, fluid rhyme.
Glistening shells applaud her leaps,
While the azure ocean deeply sleeps.

Wind becomes her silent partner,
Guiding spins that grow no darker.
Shadows stretch like satin veils,
Whirling tales of vanished gales.

The horizon frames her stage,
Nature turns each dawning page.
Graceful moves in light's embrace,
Every step a tender grace.

Oceanic Pas de Deux

Tidal waves and moonlit beams,
Craft a dance in ocean dreams.
Dolphins leap in mirrored arc,
Their union forms a stunning spark.

Watery depths now come alive,
Joyous life, it does revive.
Coral and anenome sway,
Harmonizing night with day.

Barnacles on old ship’s prow,
Offer stage lights for the now.
An undersea ballet so rare,
Performed with elegance and flair.

Glistening fins and tails entwine,
Movements sync in endless line.
Every tide a practiced cue,
For this oceanic pas de deux.

Littoral Moves

Drawing lines upon the shore,
Waves rehearse their dance once more.
Foamy edges sweep and glide,
In sync with the lunar tide.

Sandpipers dart with nimble feet,
Tracing rhythms, light and fleet.
Each motion, a silent song,
In this dance where they belong.

Pebbles hum beneath their toes,
Offering sweet undertows.
Wind and water, ancient friends,
Choreographing, their bond extends.

As the sun begins to set,
Casting shadows, silhouettes.
This coastal ballet finds its close,
In gentle moves, the sea bestows.

Deep Sea Dance

Beneath the waves where visions blur,
The ocean’s secrets softly stir.
Fish in unison glide so free,
Part of an endless, deep sea spree.

Coral fans sway to the tide’s pull,
Amidst the blue, so vast and full.
Starfish twirl in a ballet grand,
Echoes dance upon the sand.

Glistening scales under moon’s light,
Dart and twist in silent flight.
Whales’ songs echo, pure romance,
This dreamscape, the deep sea dance.

Rippled Rhythms

The surface sparkles, diamond dust,
Rippling with a gentle gust.
Water's whisper in harmonic play,
Guides the way at break of day.

Soft splashes tell stories old,
Of sailors brave and treasures bold.
The water hums a soothing tune,
Under the pale light of the moon.

Tides sway in a rhythmic trance,
Nature's own, a timeless dance.
Each wave a story, each crest a song,
Rippling rhythms, endless and strong.

Marine Shuffle

Beneath sunlight’s shimmering crest,
Sea creatures find their place of rest.
Jellyfish float with graceful flair,
In an underwater, weightless air.

Crabs in sideways shuffle prance,
In sync with ocean’s gentle stance.
Schools of fish dart quick and light,
A silver dance in shadows bright.

Kelp forests sway in a gentle breeze,
Waves’ embrace in oceans' keys.
Secrets whispered from shell to shell,
Marine shuffle, where mysteries dwell.

Coasting Steps

Footprints mark the sandy shore,
Where land meets sea forevermore.
Waves kiss the land goodnight,
In a dance of endless flight.

Seagulls' cries in harmony,
With the whispering, endless sea.
Pebbles glisten under sun's gaze,
In tidal rhythms, time’s own maze.

Broken shells and driftwood sway,
In rhythm to the sea's ballet.
The coasting steps of nature's grace,
Etched forever in this sacred space.

Marine Minuet

The ocean's breeze in gentle tease,
Whispers across the waves.
Fish do twine in waltz divine,
Through coral caverns and caves.

Seahorses sway in soft ballet,
On currents cool and free.
Their spiral dance, a dreamy trance,
Beneath the azure sea.

Anemones with flowing ease
Sway in time with the tide.
Jellyfish too, in streams of blue,
Glide with elegant pride.

Schools of bright with sheer delight,
Twirl in wondrous flight.
Rays unfurl in graceful twirl,
Through shimmering beams of light.

Octopus and squid both bid,
In harmony, they play.
In twilight's hue, they bid adieu,
To marine minuet's ballet.

Saltwater Sashay

Beneath the moon's reflective glance,
Where waves perform their nightly dance,
Saltwater whispers call my name,
In nature's ancient, rhythmic game.

Steps in the sand, a fleeting trace,
Washed by ocean's cool embrace,
A sashay in the surf so free,
A dance with tides, eternally.

Stars above in silent cheer,
As salty breezes dry each tear,
In the melody of night,
Everything feels just right.

Currents weave a fluid song,
As I'm swept on waves so strong,
Echoes of the deep sea blue,
In every step I take with you.

Driftwood dreams and moonlit rays,
Guide my nights and fill my days,
In this saltwater sashay,
I find peace in Nature's sway.

Tidal Song

Upon a shore of shifting sands,
Where waves meet land with gentle hands,
The ocean sings its lullaby,
Beneath the sprawling twilight sky.

Each wave a verse of ancient lore,
A story told from sea to shore,
Of creatures vast and journeys long,
The ocean's never-ending song.

Tides roll in with steady grace,
To brush the earth, a soft embrace,
With melodies of deep, dark blue,
They whisper secrets old and true.

Seagulls cry and breezes sigh,
A symphony beneath the sky,
In every rush and gentle pause,
Hear the sea's unending cause.

Moonlit ripples, starlit swells,
Echoes formed in ocean wells,
In this tidal song, I find,
A harmony of heart and mind.

Waves of Grace

In morning's light, the waves do shine,
With grace so pure, a sight divine,
They mirror sky and break with ease,
A dance of water in the breeze.

Each wave a whisper, soft and clear,
A message for the heart to hear,
Of strength and beauty intertwined,
In every crest and trough I find.

Ocean's arms, they pull, they push,
In silence, then a roaring rush,
A rhythm centuries in the making,
A force relentless, never breaking.

Footprints on the sandy shore,
Are touched by waves forever more,
Each mark of presence washed anew,
A testament, the sea's review.

In every rolling, graceful wave,
The ocean teaches hearts to brave,
Through storms and stillness, we embrace,
The boundless spirit of this place.

Dancing in the Tide

Toes dipped in the ocean's chill,
A heartbeat in the rhythm's thrill,
Dancing in the tide we go,
Where water ebbs and spirits flow.

Sunset's glow on waves refracted,
In every step, we're more attracted,
To liquid lullabies so sweet,
That guide our swaying, rhythmic feet.

Tidal pulls and moonlit beams,
Join our laughter, floating dreams,
In the unity of night and sea,
We find a perfect harmony.

Breezes weave through playful strands,
Of seaweed near the shore's fine sands,
With each turn and joyful leap,
We wake the ocean from its sleep.

In the tide's embrace, we glide,
No place to hide, no need for pride,
Dancing freely, hearts unlocked,
In the gentle waves, time's clock.

Ocean's Minuet

Waves whisper secrets ancient and deep,
Moonlit paths where the mermaids weep.
Salt-kissed air, a lullaby sweet,
Nature's dance beneath our feet.

Foamy fingers caress the sand,
Echoes from a distant land.
Songs of sirens call us near,
In the night, their voices clear.

The tide, a rhythm ever true,
Guides the vessels that bid adieu.
Endless horizon, blue on blue,
Mysteries vast, old and new.

Riffs of the Rockpool

Beneath the ebbing tide's soft song,
Where stars of sand and pebbles throng,
A dance of crabs, the seaweed swayed,
Their silent symphony portrayed.

Anemones like trumpets flare,
Corals whisper, if you dare,
Shells that glisten, waves that bind,
Nature's music, deeply intertwined.

Hermit homes in quiet quest,
Little fishes, colors dressed,
Rocks that echo tales untold,
Secrets in the pool unfold.

Waves that serenade the shore,
Crashing softly, evermore,
Harmony in salty air,
A lullaby beyond compare.

The light refracts in watery riffs,
Creating patterns, playful shifts,
In every corner, magic weaves,
In rockpools where the ocean breathes.

Shelled Waltz

Upon the shore, a treasure trove,
Shells gather where the tides rove.
Nature's art in shapes so quaint,
In their beauty, hearts grow faint.

Each shell tells a tale so old,
Of ocean depths and currents bold.
Swirling patterns, colors bright,
Captured in the morning light.

Ebb and flow, a gentle tune,
Beneath the whispering dunes.
Waltzing with the waves so free,
A harmony eternally.

Coastal Boogie

Beneath the moon's soft silver glow,
The ocean's waves begin to flow,
In rhythmic sways, the sand they kiss,
A dance of nature, pure and bliss.

Seagulls twirl in twilight's gleam,
Their shadows play, a gentle dream,
Waves keep time in perfect beat,
The shore becomes a ballroom suite.

Starfish waltz in tidal pools,
With barnacles as their dancing tools,
Seaweed sways in emerald flairs,
Draped in ocean's grand affairs.

Footsteps in the sand align,
To nature's music, so divine,
Barefoot dancers feel the thrill,
Of coastal boogie, wild and still.

Under starlit canopy,
The sea's own silent jubilee,
Every breeze and wave, a song,
In coastal boogie, we belong.

Crustacean Footprints

Across the sands at morning's crest,
In fleeting tracks, they made their quest,
Tiny trails of life so small,
Their journeys etched where shadows fall.

Crabs in clusters, side by side,
Leave their imprints with the tide,
A maze of marks, a story told,
Of ancient rhythms, brave and bold.

The waves erase their fleeting prints,
Gone with whispers, salty hints,
Yet in our hearts, the paths remain,
Of crustacean dancers on the plain.

In solitude, the beach is wide,
Yet life moves on the rolling tide,
Every footprint tells a tale,
In hushed tones where the oceans hail.

Soft impressions in the sand,
Patterns drawn by nature's hand,
In crustacean wander, free,
Forever marked by shores and sea.

Aqua Ballet

Beneath the waves, a dance ensues,
Marine life in varied hues.
Coral gardens, colors blaze,
In this undersea ballet.

Schools of fish in rhythm glide,
Twisting, turning with the tide.
Seaweed sways, a verdant sheet,
Choreographed by the ocean's beat.

Dolphins leap, a joyful arc,
Through the waters, leaving a mark.
In this realm where dreams alight,
Grace and wonder fill the night.

Shuffles in the Sand

Barefoot wanderers take their stroll,
Where waves caress and oceans roll,
Silent whispers of the sea,
Guide their steps in mystery.

Sand beneath their toes does shift,
With every step, a gentle lift,
A dance in nature's grand domain,
Where time is lost and bliss is gained.

Seashells glisten, pearls of white,
In moon's embrace, in soft twilight,
Each step a note in sandy song,
A harmony to which they belong.

Dunes that rise and gently fall,
Echo laughter's distant call,
Footsteps blend in patterned trails,
Stories woven by the gales.

In twilight's glow, on shores they stand,
Endless shuffles in the sand,
A journey shared, hand in hand,
Between the sea and verdant land.

Shell-Dwellers' Dance

On ocean's floor where shadows prance,
Shell-dwellers join in graceful dance.
With coral reefs as their backdrop,
They waltz in tides that never stop.

Their homes of spiral, hue and gleam,
Twirl in a silent, dreamy theme.
In the moon's soft, pearly light,
They celebrate the quiet night.

Among the anemones' blooms,
They find their rhythm, banish glooms.
Each step a tale of ancient lore,
Echoes from the ocean's core.

From dawn till dusk, their dance is long,
A symphony of silent song.
As waves compose a gentle tune,
They sway beneath a watching moon.

Beachfront Sway

Upon the golden sands we lay,
Whispers of the ocean's sway.
Palms above in rhythmic cheer,
Nature's dance is ever near.

Waves embrace the shore with grace,
Carving patterns, life's embrace.
Footprints tell of joy and strife,
Woven in the dance of life.

Seashells sing with whispers faint,
A melody that dreams paint.
In the sunlight's warm caress,
Find solace in the beach's dress.

As twilight creeps with shadows long,
The beachfront hums a soothing song.
Stars above in silent trance,
Witness to the ocean's dance.

Tidal Tempos

The tide's embrace, a rhythmic sweep,
Waves that whisper secrets deep.
In the pulse of ocean's heart,
Find the tempos of each part.

Sand and sea in constant play,
Mark the passage of each day.
Ebb and flow, a ceaseless beat,
Where water, sky, and shoreline meet.

Moon pulls strings from high above,
Guiding dances that we love.
In the night, the waves do hum,
Tidal tempos softly strum.

Rock pools glisten in the light,
Reflecting stars on tranquil nights.
Their gentle ripples form a song,
In tidal tempos we belong.

Dormant Dance

In silent fields where shadows glide,
Dormant seeds of dreams reside.
Beneath the earth, a dance unknown,
Life awaits in hushed tone.

Winter's breath upon the land,
Choreographs a sleep so grand.
Yet below, in slumber deep,
Roots and wishes softly keep.

As spring whispers her return,
Dormant dancers start to learn.
Shoots of green and buds of bloom,
Break the silent, quiet gloom.

From dormant sleep to life's embrace,
Nature's dance begins with grace.
Every seed, a hidden chance,
Wakes to join the verdant dance.

Nighttime Coastal Rhythm

Soft whispers of the twilight breeze,
Rustling through the ancient trees.
Under stars, the ocean sighs,
Reflecting dreams in endless skies.

Moonlight dances on gentle waves,
Illuminates hidden oceanic caves.
Each crest a melody in flight,
A symphony in the still of night.

Footprints vanish in the sand,
As tides reclaim their rightful land.
Starlit shadows come to play,
Dusk and dawn, a lovely sway.

Secrets of the Seafloor

Beneath the azure waves' gentle lore,
Mysteries lie on the ocean's floor.
Sunlight fades in depths cold and deep,
Where ancient whispers softly sleep.

Coral castles in shadows rest,
Guardians of secrets, nature's best.
Eons etched in shells and sand,
Legends spun by a timeless hand.

Wonders thrive in silence profound,
Creatures rare, the unseen astound.
Mermaids' sighs and triton's call,
Echo secrets hidden from all.

Volcanic kisses, molten flow,
Shape the realms down far below.
Beneath the calm, the storm concealed,
In darkness, life's truth revealed.

Ceaseless tides keep secrets close,
In the abyss where mysteries pose.
An unseen world so rich and deep,
Where the ocean's deepest secrets sleep.

Underwater Ballet

In depths where silence softly sways,
A ballet of fluid grace,
Fishes glide in gentle plays,
Nature's dancers interlace.

Seagrass waves in fleeting steps,
Ripples mark the fleeting beat,
Eels emerge from hidden reps,
Shells applaud with sand-soft feet.

Colors blend in liquid light,
Curving through the ocean's tune,
Every move a sheer delight,
Beneath the silver-framed moon.

Salty Steps

Waves dance lightly on golden sand,
Painting stories with nature's hand.
Barefoot steps in patterns weave,
Traces that the sea will leave.

Salty mist on lips' embrace,
Hints of journeys, a fleeting trace.
Every step a song of old,
Echoes of tales left untold.

Footprints kissed by morning tide,
Waltzing with the ocean wide.
Rhythms of the breaking foam,
Sing of wanderers' endless roam.

Seagulls glide on the breezy air,
To melodies beyond compare.
Each wave a verse, each breeze a line,
In this poetic shoreline shrine.

Where sea and sand together blend,
In harmony they transcend.
Salty steps on shifting shore,
Whisper of adventures more.

Oceanic Waltz

Beneath the moon's tranquil light,
Oceans waltz in the quiet night.
Waves caress the silent shore,
In rhythms ancient, forevermore.

Stars above in glistening dance,
Reflect on waters' soft expanse.
Mermaids twirl with evening’s tide,
In liquid corridors, side by side.

Coral gardens sway in tune,
To melodies sung by the moon.
Fish in colors bright and bold,
Join the waltz with magic untold.

Currents carry whispers sweet,
In this waltz where worlds meet.
Whales sing with voices deep,
In the ocean's arms, dreams sleep.

Harmony in liquid grace,
Across the depths, a vast embrace.
Waltz of waves in twilight's hue,
Oceanic dance, ever true.

Beachfront Shuffle

Here along the sun-kissed coast,
Children's laughter fills the air,
Each small step a joyful boast,
Beachfront shuffle, without care.

Crabs perform a sidelong dance,
Clicking claws in rhythmic schemes,
In the shuffle, there's a chance,
To live within these sandy dreams.

Shells lay out in patterned rows,
Nature's carpet at our feet,
Every shuffle the heart knows,
Summer's tune, so pure and sweet.

Tidal Two-Step

Against the shore, tides rise and fall,
Nature's dance, the ocean's call.
Steps in rhythm, ebb and flow,
Symphony in moonlight's glow.

Beach and sea in close embrace,
Twin steps in eternal chase.
Seashells echo songs of old,
Stories in the sands retold.

Frothy edges mark the beat,
Dance of water, sand beneath.
Crabs and clams join in the show,
With tides, they come and go.

Dolphins leap in joyous flight,
Under skies of twilight light.
In this dance of liquid grace,
Countless lives find their place.

Tidal steps, a dance so grand,
Boundless waltz on sea and land.
Nature’s dance, forever bright,
In the two-step's gentle might.

Marine Choreography

Waves compose a silent score,
Currents guide the unseen hand,
Dolphins weave in arcs of lore,
Choreographed across the sand.

Turtle's spin with ancient grace,
Echoing a timeless script,
Patterns traced in endless space,
Watercraft so finely clipped.

Coral blooms in artful lines,
Every shade a note so rare,
In this dance, beyond confines,
Ocean sings its boundless air.

Coastal Pirouette

On the shore where sea meets land,
Footprints mark a transient tale,
Dancers of the tides expand,
Moves unravel in the gale.

Sandpipers chase the receding surf,
With nimble steps and beak-touched sand,
Their synchronized turns give birth,
To fleeting marks that grace the strand.

The sun dips low, a golden end,
Mirroring their final spin,
Nature and art blend and blend,
In pirouettes that whirl within.

Rhythms of the Reef

Beneath the ocean's gentle sway,
Corals bloom in bright array,
Fish in colors, bold and grand,
Dance across the sandy strand.

Whispers of the waters deep,
Secrets that the seahorses keep,
Turtles glide through liquid blue,
Amid the kelp, where dreams come true.

Anemones with tendrils wide,
Offer refuge, where creatures hide,
The reef's a kingdom, wild and bright,
A world of wonder, day and night.

Echoes of a distant song,
In this paradise, we all belong,
Stars reflect in waves that crest,
The rhythms of the reef, never rest.

Crabs and shrimps along the floor,
Navigate to find much more,
A symphony in azure hues,
Nature's symphony, vast and true.

Crustacean Cadence

Crabs march sideways on the shore,
In perfect timing, evermore,
Their claws click in rhythmic beat,
A coastal cadence, pure and sweet.

Lobsters in their armored suits,
Move through waters, resolute,
Their antennae feel the way,
In the ocean's grand ballet.

Shrimps in shallows, dart with grace,
A myriad in a hidden place,
Their motions quick, an artful show,
In the currents' ebb and flow.

Barnacles on rocks, steadfast,
Hold their ground as waves rush past,
Their lives in sync with tidal sweep,
In nature's cradle, calm and deep.

Crustaceans in their endless dance,
Move with purpose, take a chance,
Under moonlight, stars above,
Echoes of an ancient love.

Crescent Shore Dancers

Moonlight casts its silver sheen,
Upon the waves, serene and keen,
Where dolphins leap and gulls do soar,
In dance along the crescent shore.

Footprints fade upon the sand,
Erased by tides' gentle hand,
Seashells sing a quiet tune,
Beneath the gaze of a rising moon.

Sandpipers in a synchronized flight,
Flit in shadows of the night,
Their forms create an artful scene,
Of elegance few have seen.

Breezes hum a soothing tone,
Where starfish lay, soft as stone,
Each motion tells a timeless tale,
In this tranquil coastal vale.

Waves caress the sleepy shore,
Secrets told forever more,
In dances lit by lunar glow,
Nature's ballet in ebb and flow.

Coastal Rhythms

Waves crash with a thunderous might,
Breaking into foamy white,
Ebb and flow, a constant beat,
A symphony at our feet.

Seagulls call in morning light,
Their wings in effortless flight,
Skirting edges of the sea,
In their coastal melody.

Tides retreat and then return,
As lanterns of the heavens burn,
Shores are kissed by liquid breath,
In a dance of life and death.

Pebbles polished by the swell,
Stories that the currents tell,
Driftwood whispers ancient lore,
Treasures washed upon the shore.

Each day dawns with a new refrain,
Echoes of the sea remain,
In the heartbeats of the waves,
Coastal rhythms, oceanic staves.

Marine Magicians

Beneath the waves where secrets lie,
Creatures swim in hues that fly,
In coral reefs, they weave and die,
A spell of life beneath the sky.

Octopus paints with ink so black,
Sharks patrol, they watch their back,
Anglerfish with lights that track,
A dance of shadows in the slack.

Jellyfish with skeletal grace,
Glide through currents, set the pace,
Seahorses in love's embrace,
In this world, there's no disgrace.

Starfish cling to rocks and stay,
Crabs with sideways steps at bay,
Eels in caverns hide away,
Marine magicians, night and day.

Dolphins leap with joyful cries,
Whales sing songs to pierce the skies,
In the deep where mystery lies,
This ocean kingdom never dies.

Coastal Cadence

Rolling tides that shimmer bright,
Reflect the day's diminishing light,
The sand beneath feels cool at night,
A rhythmic pulse, a breathing sight.

Gulls above in winding flight,
Call to waves in pure delight,
Driftwood whispers tales of might,
In coastal cadence, hearts unite.

Shells that tell of distant lands,
Found within our reaching hands,
Footprints trace our earthly plans,
Lost to time, to shifting sands.

Salted breezes sweep the shore,
Echoing of ages yore,
Waves compose a peaceful lore,
A song that sings forevermore.

Lighthouses that touch the sky,
Guide the ships with beaconed eye,
In this place where sea meets dry,
Coastal cadence, never shy.

Dancing on Ocean Floors

In the depths where light is sparse,
Creatures move in silent arcs,
Echoes of a faint sonar,
Dancing on the ocean floor.

Soft corals sway as currents flow,
In a lightless, silent show,
Bioluminescent glows,
Reveal the steps, the undertow.

Shells in spirals, interesting forms,
Witness to the deep-sea norms,
Fishes dance through gentle storms,
In these dark, secluded dorms.

Giant squid with tentacles wide,
Gracefully through waters glide,
In their movements, do confide,
Mysteries of the oceans wide.

Anemones in vibrant hues,
Sway like dancers with soft cues,
In this ballroom of the blues,
Dancing on the ocean floors.

Sideways Movements

Crabs make way with sideways stride,
Through the brine-touched sands they ride,
In their armor, there’s no pride,
Just a journey side to side.

Shrimp with bent and crooked paths,
Dodge the lurking, hungry wraths,
Sideways movements in their maths,
Safe within the water's baths.

Fiddler crabs with claws held high,
Pincer wars beneath the sky,
In the surf they bid goodbye,
Waves their always-present ally.

Seals on beaches stretch and yawn,
Move with grace as night meets dawn,
On their bellies, they are drawn,
Sideways movements, nature's pawn.

Waves themselves in slanted race,
Slide across the sandy face,
In each crest a sideways chase,
Harmony in slanted grace.

Underwater Escapade

In a realm beneath the waves,
Where sunlight shyly braves,
A world of whispers softly greets,
With hidden pearls and coral fleets.

We dive through blue's embrace,
Ancient secrets we efface,
Amongst the kelp, we drift and play,
In pure serenity, we stay.

Fish in colors bright and bold,
Dance in harmony, tales untold,
A silent ballet, a quiet cheer,
In depths where dreams appear.

The ocean’s heart, a rhythmic beat,
Where salt and sky and sea all meet,
We lose ourselves in azure trance,
In fluid grace, a timeless dance.

Emerging to the surface high,
We bid the deep a fond goodbye,
To land resurgent, but forever called,
By underwater spirits enthralled.

Ocean's Footsteps

Where the shore meets ocean's crest,
Each step is but a humble guest,
In the symphony of rise and fall,
Nature's whispers softly call.

Footprints lead to water’s edge,
With promises the tides allege,
A journey carved in grains of sand,
By mysteries unseen, unplanned.

Beneath the moon’s ethereal glow,
The sea reflects what stars bestow,
Each wave a sigh, a soft caress,
An echo of the heart's finesse.

Upon the breeze, the song is clear,
A melody both far and near,
In ocean’s footsteps, one can find,
A solace for the wandering mind.

As twilight fades to softest hue,
Ocean’s tales feel ever new,
In every footprint, every trace,
Lies the ocean’s vast embrace.

Marine Refrain

Within the ocean's vast domain,
Lies a haunting, soft refrain,
A melody both wild and free,
Whispered secrets of the sea.

Ebb and flow, the tune persists,
In every crest and trough exists,
A rhythm born of moon's command,
Cradled in the sea's vast hand.

The dolphins play in joyous spree,
Their laughter punctuates the sea,
In harmony they weave their part,
A symphony from nature’s heart.

Beneath the waves, the whispers blend,
In currents deep, the echoes send,
A song that’s felt and heard through time,
An endless, boundless, fluid rhyme.

In silence, as the day does wane,
List to the marine refrain,
For in its notes, a truth is spun,
Of life's refrain, the sea and sun.

Shoreline Elegance

By the shore where dreams reside,
In elegance, the waves abide,
A dance of grace on sandy stage,
Nature’s beauty, wisdom sage.

The tide’s embrace, a lover’s kiss,
In each caress, a fleeting bliss,
Whispers of a world unseen,
In hues of blue and emerald green.

Seagulls call with voices clear,
Their melodies both far and near,
Above the shoreline’s soft parade,
In skies where freedom’s fate is made.

The shells that garnish ocean’s rim,
Each speaks a tale, a secret hymn,
Of journeys past and lives once known,
In elegant repose, they’ve grown.

As twilight paints the sky’s expanse,
In golden hues, the waves advance,
By shores adorned in silent grace,
We find our hearts in nature’s place.

Crustacean Rhythms

In the depths where shadows blend,
Crabs and lobsters, they descend,
Their claws tap in rhythmic play,
Beneath the ocean's grand ballet.

Sheltered by the coral's grace,
They move in time and leave no trace,
A hidden dance beneath the foam,
The seafloor beads become their home.

Crusty shells with stories told,
Ancient rhythms, ages old,
Echoes of a deep lagoon,
Beneath the stars, beneath the moon.

Waters whisper secrets low,
To those who in the deep below,
Understand the rhythm's call,
Crustacean dances, one and all.

Tide and current, ebb and flow,
Guide where these creatures go,
In the delicate balance of the sea,
A crustacean rhythm, wild and free.

Currents and Crawls

Beneath the waves, in caverns deep,
Where ancient mariners do sleep,
Currents whisper tales untold,
Of crawlers seeking treasures bold.

Green and blue, a shifting hue,
Through kelp forests, creeping crew,
Soft and silent, shadow's drift,
Following the ocean's lift.

Softly scuttle through the sand,
Processes that nature planned,
In ocean's grasp, they find their way,
Through the night and through the day.

Mysteries of salt and brine,
Outlined by the currents' spine,
Creeping creatures mark their path,
Through the deep seas' ancient bath.

Beneath the surf, the world below,
Lives in currents' gentle flow,
With every crawl, a tale is spun,
In the deep, where life's begun.

Shellfish Serenade

Silence sings in ocean’s deep,
Where shellfish secrets often keep,
A serenade of whispering tones,
In coral castles, ancient stones.

Oysters murmur soft and low,
As clams beneath the currents grow,
A symphony of growing shells,
In watery realms where magic dwells.

Mussels cling to rocky shore,
An echoed song of evermore,
Their lullabies of ocean’s glide,
In harmony the seas provide.

In twilight's hues, a gentle hum,
From shellfish throats, so sweetly strum,
Their serenade, a soft embrace,
In ocean’s ballroom, finding place.

Listen to their gentle croon,
Beneath the silvery, watching moon,
A serenade that does not fade,
Beneath the waves, it's gently laid.

Neptune's Waltz

In Neptune's hall of water grand,
Where dreams and reality blend,
A waltz begins so slow and true,
Beneath the ocean's royal blue.

Seahorses prance with graceful bends,
Along the currents' gentle trends,
Their partners are the schools of fish,
Dancing to the deep sea's wish.

The whales' song sets the rhythm right,
Guiding dancers through the night,
In Neptune's waltz, they find their beat,
Ancient steps with melody sweet.

Anemones sway with every tone,
Their colors cast in coral stone,
A ballroom vast, with endless flow,
Where ocean's creatures ebb and grow.

Join the dance beneath the tide,
Where Neptune's waltz will ever guide,
A symphony of life and grace,
In the ocean's grand embrace.

Ebb and Flow Tango

The moon pulls threads of silver light,
Guiding waves in twilight's dance,
A seascape draped in tranquil night,
With tides that rise in sweet romance.

In cadence, whispers of the sea,
Embrace the shores with tender grace,
A rhythm ancient, wild, and free,
In liquid waltz, they interlace.

The ocean's breath, a soft caress,
Each wave, a kiss upon the sand,
A dance of love in timelessness,
Led by the moon's celestial hand.

Ebb beckons to the tender flow,
In moments lost, in currents found,
A symphony of high and low,
Their tango's song, a sacred sound.

So let us join this ocean's rite,
With hearts as vast as skies above,
And in the music of the night,
We'll find the steps of endless love.

Beachside Ballet

On the shore, where waves do play,
Golden sands in bright array,
Seagulls glide in vast display,
Nature's dance, a fine ballet.

Shells and stones along the way,
Sunset hues in soft bouquet,
Stars emerge, both near and far,
Moonlight's glow, a gentle star.

Water's edge, a whisper's sway,
Tidal rhythms hold their say,
Footprints mark where dreams once lay,
Ephemeral, they fade away.

Crustacean Choreography

Beneath the waves, where secrets dwell,
The crustaceans take the stage,
In ocean's hush, they weave a spell,
With claws and shells, a silent page.

The lobsters twist in regal glide,
Crabs scuttle in precise array,
In rhythm with the shifting tide,
A dance unseen by light of day.

Their movements tell of ancient lore,
Of currents deep and mysteries,
Each step a part of ocean's score,
In whispered tones of prophecies.

Against the sand, they etch their art,
In patterns grand, a living show,
A tale that speaks to every heart,
Of life in ebb, and life in flow.

So watch the sea with patient eyes,
Find beauty in each subtle sway,
For in its depths, the choreo lies,
A dance to grace both night and day.

Crustacean Capers

In the sand, what scuttles there?
Crabs in dance, without a care,
Tiny legs, a merry pair,
Shoreline’s jesters, light as air.

Hermits drag their borrowed homes,
On their backs, the sea foam roams,
In the nooks and tidal domes,
Where the ocean's secret looms.

Claws that click in twilight gleam,
Underneath the starlit beam,
Crustacean capers, like a dream,
Ocean’s jesters, in their theme.

Tidepool Ballet

In tidal pools, where dreams collect,
Tiny dancers start their plight,
With every step and spin, reflect,
The gentle whispers of the night.

Anemones in gowns so bright,
Sway softly in the ocean's breeze,
They bend and curl in pale moonlight,
In liquid steps that aim to please.

The starfish spread in graceful arcs,
Their limbs a choreography,
With subtle moves, they leave their marks,
In water's silent symphony.

The shadows flicker, life abounds,
Each creature finds its waiting place,
In mirrored depths, their world surrounds,
A ballet spun with tender grace.

Observe the dance below the waves,
A world of twirls and pirouettes,
For nature's stage, where ocean paves,
Their tidepool ballet never rests.

Strolls in Sand

Barefoot paths on golden shore,
Where the sea’s embrace is sure,
Every step a whispered lore,
Ancient tales, yearning for more.

Dunes rise high, a sandy crest,
Seashells tucked in nature's chest,
Glistening waves that never rest,
Ocean's breath, at its best.

Sun and wind, a duet grand,
Hand in hand, we walk the strand,
In the silence, moments spanned,
Life and time, grains of sand.

Sandy Pirouettes

On sandy shores where dreams are spun,
The dancers of the sea behold,
In morning light or setting sun,
Their sandy pirouettes unfold.

The seagulls glide in arcs so high,
Their wings that brush the sky's pure blue,
In echo with the ocean's sigh,
They spin a tale both old and new.

Small hermits in their borrowed homes,
Perform a waltz upon the beach,
In every shell, the chorus roams,
A dance within each tidal reach.

The gentle breeze lends nature's song,
To every step, a sweet caress,
Their movements in the sands prolong,
A dance of pure, unspokenness.

So watch the show upon the shore,
Where nature's elegance is set,
The sandy stage forever more,
Where dancers whirl in pirouette.

Intertidal Tango

In the realm where waters meet,
Rocky pools at our feet,
Creatures small, a hidden fleet,
In their dance, rhythms sweet.

Barnacles and mussels cling,
To the stone with mighty swing,
Waves compose, the sea does sing,
Nature's ballet, offering.

Fish dart in a fluid lane,
In this world of brine and rain,
Intertidal dance remains,
Forever free, never tamed.

Shell-backed Dancers

Upon the golden sands they twirl,
Their patterns weave, their figures swirl,
In timeless dance under the sky,
With silent grace, they move and fly.

Beneath the waves, a world unseen,
In crystal depths, with blue serene,
They waltz to realms where light refrains,
Through coral halls and watery lanes.

By moonlit beams and stars aglow,
Their rhythms hush, their currents flow,
They lead the dance from shore to sea,
With every step, wild, bold, and free.

In pearly shells their tales reside,
Of ancient dreams where oceans bide,
They whisper songs of ocean's lore,
As time cascades forevermore.

Eternal dancers, endless sway,
In ocean's arms they spend their day,
Shell-backed companions of the deep,
In waves of blue, their secrets keep.

Coastal Pirouettes

By sandy banks where tides embrace,
They twirl with unmatched, fluid grace,
Their movements weave a tale of yore,
In maritime ballets on the shore.

The sea's soft whisper guides their feet,
In rhythm to the gull's heartbeat,
Each pirouette, a liquid note,
In nature's symphony, they float.

Their stage, the boundless ocean's seam,
The sunlight casts its golden gleam,
They spin through morning's gentle rise,
And dance beneath the azure skies.

With every wave, a leap of faith,
In gentle arcs, they sketch a wraith,
A fleeting wisp of ocean's breath,
In joyful dance, defying death.

As twilight falls, their dance begins,
With stars they weave their secret hymns,
Coastal dancers, night and day,
In eternal pirouettes, they sway.

Shoreline Steps

Upon the edge where sea meets land,
Their footprints trace the golden sand,
With every wave, a tender kiss,
In shoreline steps, boundless bliss.

They wade through dawn's first gentle light,
With rhythmic steps, both soft and light,
Each move a testament to grace,
In nature's dance, they find their place.

The whispers of the ebbing tide,
Guide gently where their spirits glide,
In steps that paint the ocean's tune,
A dance beneath the sun and moon.

With seagulls as their serenade,
And wind the lyrics, ocean-made,
They step through realms of blue and white,
In graceful arcs, both day and night.

Their journey framed by wave and shore,
In every turn, they seek no more,
Than simple dance to nature's beat,
Where sea and land in rhythm meet.

Pelagic Pavan

In deep cerulean halls they glide,
Through realms where ancient secrets hide,
A pavan to the ocean's song,
With measured steps, serene and long.

Their movements, slow yet full of grace,
In silent waters, find their place,
Through currents mild, their forms entwine,
In dances where the salt waves shine.

The deep abyss, a mystic floor,
Where shadows drift and fathoms soar,
Their fluid steps a tranquil play,
In ocean's depths, they greet the day.

With bioluminescent glow,
They trace paths only dreamers know,
A ballet in the ocean's keep,
Where time dissolves in waters deep.

Ethereal dancers of the sea,
In pavan's flow, they wander free,
Their silent waltz an endless rhyme,
In pelagic dance, beyond all time.

Seabed Patterns

On the seabed, mysteries lie,
Tales whispered by the shy.
Corals paint a vibrant hue,
Silent dancers in the blue.

Shells that sparkle, lost in time,
Echo songs in ocean's chime.
Patterns weave a quilt of grace,
Nature's art in hidden space.

Fish, like brushstrokes, weave and dart,
Each a masterpiece of art.
Waves caress the sandy bed,
Dreams afloat on waters spread.

Glimmers caught in sunlight's beam,
Underwater, life's a dream.
In the depths where stillness reigns,
Beauty surges through the veins.

Rippling Rhythms

Beneath the surface, ripples wend,
In rhythms that the waters send.
Moonlit paths on oceans wide,
Guiding tides like time’s true guide.

Ebbing flows, the heart's own beat,
Mingling with the current's sweep.
Secrets carried far and near,
Whispered truths for those who hear.

Gentle waves that kiss the shore,
Leave imprints that ask for more.
Nature’s lullaby and lore,
Dreams awash in ocean’s core.

Ripples dance in soft ballet,
Patterns fleeting in their play.
Mirrored skies above they trace,
Echoes of a tranquil grace.

Marine Waltz

Beneath the frothy, tireless waves,
Where light and shadow interlace.
Creatures swirling, spirits high,
In a timeless waltz they fly.

Seahorses and angels fair,
Twirl in the aquatic air.
Waltzing to the oceans' beat,
Graceful fins and flippers meet.

Starry skies and moon's soft glow,
Guide this dance where dreams flow.
Marine life in nightly thrall,
Echoes in the ocean hall.

Ballet of the endless seas,
Silent songs in minor keys.
Harmony in every glance,
Nature's grand, eternal dance.

Ocean's Sashay

Beneath the sun's warm, radiant beam,
Waves sashay in a choreographed dream.
Sparkling diamonds on water’s face,
Nature’s dance, a fluid grace.

Gentle swirls in endless blue,
In the dance, perspectives new.
Foam tipped toes, the water’s ballet,
Ocean’s secrets on display.

Rhythm in the ocean’s beat,
Where the sky and water meet.
Every wave a poet’s pen,
Writes a story, then again.

Twilight’s kiss on ocean’s edge,
Moonlight glows like silken pledge.
Dancing tides in night’s array,
Stars reflecting ocean's sashay.

In the ebb and flow we find,
A dance eternal, undefined.
Ocean’s sashay, timeless play,
Nature’s ballet, night and day.

Coastal Glide

Where land and ocean gently kiss,
There lies a world of gentle bliss.
Tides that wash on sandy shores,
Stories told of yesteryores.

Waves that rise and softly break,
Songs the coastal winds do make.
Seagulls cry above the spray,
Endless dance in night and day.

Footprints tracing paths of time,
Moments captured, oh sublime.
Driftwood whispers tales unsaid,
Secrets of the ocean bed.

Soft horizon meets the eyes,
Blending seas with endless skies.
In this glide where worlds unite,
Coast and ocean, pure delight.

Tidal Elegance

Waves whisper secrets, in moonlit embrace,
Their timeless rhythm, a dance of grace.
Silvery trails, where stars dip low,
In ocean's depth, soft currents flow.

Ebb and flow, the tide's quiet song,
To this ancient cadence, we belong.
Footprints vanish in sands of light,
Only to return with morning's flight.

Shells and stones, with stories untold,
Glimmer in hues, of purple and gold.
Each wave a brush, on nature's art,
In each drop, the ocean's heart.

Moonlight glows on tranquil seas,
Whispers of the nocturnal breeze.
In the silence, a symphony plays,
Quiet beauty of night's embrace.

Eternal dance of sea and sky,
Bound by tides that never lie.
In tidal elegance, we find,
A timeless peace, a tranquil mind.

Shoreside Harmony

Glistening sands beneath the skies,
Where the sea meets morning's rise.
Gulls in flight, call out in glee,
Echoes of waves, in harmony.

Salt air sings with the breaking dawn,
Day's new light upon the lawn.
Ripples whisper tales untold,
Of journeys and treasures bold.

Azure waves with white caps crest,
On rocky shores they come to rest.
Each wave a note in nature's song,
Where land and ocean do belong.

Palm trees sway in breeze's hand,
Drawing pictures in the sand.
Nature's choir, a sweet refrain,
In every tide, joy and pain.

Reflections dance on water's face,
Endless bond, a warm embrace.
In shoreside harmony, we see,
A timeless dance of unity.

Shelled Symphony

Hidden in the sands below,
Shells that catch the sunlight's glow.
Each one sings in quiet tone,
A symphony in seashells' home.

Waves compose the music here,
Notes of water, crisp and clear.
Nature's score, so pure, refined,
In shelled beauty, peace we find.

Tides reveal a shining band,
Ocean's treasures in one's hand.
Colors blend in hallowed peace,
In their stillness, struggles cease.

Children's laughter, mingles near,
Joining nature's hymn so dear.
Harmony in every crest,
An ocean's heart laid to rest.

Gathered shells, a memory,
Of ocean's tunes, a melody.
Shelled symphony, serene and grand,
Crafted by nature's gentle hand.

Intertidal Intricacies

The tide recedes, revealing glistening sand,
Where clams and crabs in hidden silence stand.
Between the waves, life's secrets lie,
In shallow pools beneath the azure sky.

Barnacles cling to the rocks so tight,
Seaweed dances in the soft twilight.
Anemones bloom with colors bright,
In intertidal worlds, time feels right.

Starfish crawl in their starry grace,
Leaving trails that the currents erase.
Waves bring whispers from the deep,
Stories the ocean keeps in sleep.

Each footprint washed, no trace remains,
Nature's art in cyclic refrains.
The rhythm of tides, a ceaseless song,
In intertidal areas, we belong.

Eclectic life in the shifting zone,
A universe within our own.
Where sea and land in harmony blend,
Forever changing, yet no end.

Shell Game Serenade

On the shore where the oceans meet,
Shells tell tales of where they've been.
Patterns painted by the sea,
A mosaic of life, wild and free.

Tiny homes of creatures past,
In the sand they find their last.
Castoff treasures, white and gray,
Songs of waves, their serenade play.

Hermit crabs with homes on backs,
Scuttle across with no known tracks.
Shells of innocence, shelters found,
A simple beauty all around.

Collect them in a child's hand,
Shells that whisper, shells that stand.
Each with stories, old and new,
Silent echoes in the blue.

A symphony of shell and shore,
A melody, forevermore.
In the shell game, life's parade,
Nature’s notes so finely made.

Claw Caper

Crab scuttles sideways on the beach,
Claws that snap within their reach.
Silent dancers in the sand,
Playing games by nature's hand.

Under moonlight, they parade,
In a caper, unafraid.
Shells gleaming in the night,
Stars above, a guiding light.

Burrows deep where secrets lie,
In the sand beneath the sky.
Guardians of their tiny world,
In this dance, their life unfurled.

Waves crash down with rhythmic beat,
Yet the crabs, they don't retreat.
In the caper, bold and bright,
They keep moving, out of sight.

Claws and shells and sandy trails,
Tales of crabs in moonlit veils.
A caper etched on shores so wide,
In the ocean's ebb and tide.

Milton Keynes UK
Ingram Content Group UK Ltd.
UKHW022240280824
447491UK00010B/285

9 789916 864869